Scoring High

Iowa Tests of Basic Skills®

A Test Prep Program for ITBS®

Book 1
Now with Science

Columbus, OH

The **McGraw·Hill** Companies

SRAonline.com

 SRA

Send all inquiries to:
SRA/McGraw-Hill
4400 Easton Commons
Columbus, OH 43219

Printed in the United States of America.

ISBN 0-07-604364-9

4 5 6 7 8 9 QPD 09 08

The **McGraw·Hill** Companies

On Your Way to Scoring High

On the **Iowa Tests of Basic Skills**®

Name _____

Unit 1

Vocabulary

Lesson 1a **Vocabulary Skills**

 **TIPS** Think about the meaning of the picture.

S

- ○ swim
- ○ dive
- ○ splash
- ○ float

3

- ○ rake
- ○ broom
- ○ mop
- ○ shovel

1

- ○ frown
- ○ yawn
- ○ groan
- ○ wink

4

- ○ shout
- ○ chase
- ○ catch
- ○ jump

2

- ○ scarf
- ○ leash
- ○ belt
- ○ collar

5

- ○ give
- ○ match
- ○ split
- ○ spread

GO

1

6

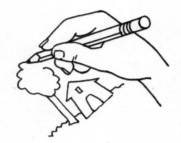

- ○ write
- ○ draw
- ○ paint
- ○ measure

9

- ○ dock
- ○ sailboat
- ○ raft
- ○ canoe

7

- ○ toss
- ○ catch
- ○ shoot
- ○ swing

10

- ○ bushy
- ○ smelly
- ○ rainy
- ○ lazy

8

- ○ sweater
- ○ jacket
- ○ vest
- ○ shirt

11

- ○ chimney
- ○ roof
- ○ window
- ○ tower

STOP

Unit 1 Vocabulary

Lesson 1b **Vocabulary Skills**

If you aren't sure which answer is correct, take your best guess.

S A place with little water is a …

- ○ forest
- ○ desert
- ○ beach
- ○ mountain

1 To be sleepy is to be …

- ○ happy
- ○ tired
- ○ quiet
- ○ cold

2 A small city is a …

- ○ park
- ○ street
- ○ farm
- ○ town

3 To keep safe is to …

- ○ finish
- ○ buy
- ○ share
- ○ protect

4 A light wind is a …

- ○ breeze
- ○ storm
- ○ cloud
- ○ sky

GO ➡

5

To make no noise is to be …

○ silent   ○ nervous   ○ silly   ○ friendly

6

To use a broom is to …

○ wait   ○ sweep   ○ wash   ○ shake

7

Someone who is very happy is …

○ loud   ○ gentle   ○ cheerful   ○ funny

8

To pick up roughly is to …

○ hide   ○ grab   ○ bend   ○ climb

9

To lie in the water is to …

○ play   ○ drink   ○ splash   ○ float

10

Something that can hurt is …

○ dangerous   ○ crowded   ○ interesting   ○ tricky

STOP

 # Unit 1

Test Yourself: Vocabulary

S

- ○ fish
- ○ spin
- ○ drift
- ○ row

3

- ○ mostly
- ○ carefully
- ○ suddenly
- ○ hardly

1

- ○ puddle
- ○ swallow
- ○ shower
- ○ kitchen

4

- ○ airplane
- ○ train
- ○ submarine
- ○ tanker

2

- ○ message
- ○ bag
- ○ letter
- ○ package

5

- ○ problem
- ○ traffic
- ○ race
- ○ game

GO ▶

6

- ○ twist
- ○ shake
- ○ squeeze
- ○ borrow

9

- ○ fry
- ○ bake
- ○ toast
- ○ slice

7

- ○ wash
- ○ scrub
- ○ wipe
- ○ mess

10

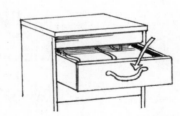

- ○ button
- ○ lock
- ○ knob
- ○ handle

8

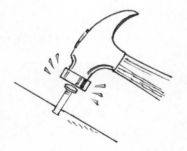

- ○ pound
- ○ knock
- ○ screw
- ○ thud

11

- ○ quilt
- ○ blanket
- ○ sheet
- ○ pillow

STOP

12

Something loud is …

○ noisy   ○ pleasant   ○ hushed   ○ busy

13

To feel rough is to be …

○ smooth   ○ fluffy   ○ scratchy   ○ thick

14

People marching in the street is a …

○ concert   ○ party   ○ race   ○ parade

15

To be scared is to be …

○ afraid   ○ cold   ○ hungry   ○ sick

16

A deep valley is a …

○ meadow   ○ river   ○ canyon   ○ tunnel

17

To look for something is to …

○ wait   ○ search   ○ dream   ○ taste

STOP

Word Analysis

Unit 2

Lesson 2a **Letter Recognition**

S1

log   big   red
○   ○   ○

S2

hat   made   fork
○   ○   ○

TIPS

Listen to the directions.

Read each answer choice carefully.

1

fine   day   fly
○   ○   ○

4

not   near   tore
○   ○   ○

2

street   slip   trade
○   ○   ○

5 🔔

did   hop   win
○   ○   ○

3

any   each   edge
○   ○   ○

6

head   west   hurt
○   ○   ○

STOP

1
oven   oil   up
○   ○   ○

6
spin   like   nine
○   ○   ○

2
broom   root   boost
○   ○   ○

7
cold   lost   cage
○   ○   ○

3
sad   yes   get
○   ○   ○

8
heart   hand   have
○   ○   ○

4
stand   sore   toss
○   ○   ○

9
load   fast   far
○   ○   ○

5
other   easy   open
○   ○   ○

10
hot   hang   here
○   ○   ○

STOP

S

teen

scr

   ○

   ○

   ○

Listen carefully to the directions.

Say the name of each picture to yourself.

1

dome

h

○   ○   ○

2

jump

p

○   ○   ○

3

down

cl

○   ○   ○

4

fair

ch

○   ○   ○

STOP

Word Analysis

Lesson 3b **Initial Sounds**

1

mess

dr

○ ○ ○

2

show

sn

○ ○ ○

3

camp

l

○ ○ ○

4

rest

n

○ ○ ○

5

make

c

○ ○ ○

6

tile

sm

○ ○ ○

STOP

11

S  __ost

l	gh	m
○	○	○

 Listen to the word and look at the picture.
Try each answer in the blank.

1  __ing

spr	sl	w
○	○	○

2  __een

s	qu	cr
○	○	○

3  __arn

g	j	y
○	○	○

STOP

S

m__tten

e	o	i
○	○	○

TIPS

Listen for the sound in the middle.

Think about the sound each answer would make in the blank.

1

b__n

oo	ea	oa
○	○	○

2

b___t

oa	ou	oi
○	○	○

3

l__ck

i	e	o
○	○	○

STOP

Word Analysis

Lesson 5a **Vowel Sounds**

S

TIPS Listen carefully for the vowel sound, the sound in the middle of the word.

1

2

3

1

tap	kind	lake
○	○	○

2

mail	pass	loud
○	○	○

3

join	burn	roar
○	○	○

4

turn	hard	born
○	○	○

5

meal	wash	bend
○	○	○

6

shall	hunt	list
○	○	○

STOP

Test Yourself: Word Analysis

Unit 2

S1

until   ant   eat
○   ○   ○

S2

hard   went   book
○   ○   ○

1

egg   art   old
○   ○   ○

5

wore   cart   want
○   ○   ○

2

of   air   ear
○   ○   ○

6

good   play   loud
○   ○   ○

3

fear   hope   date
○   ○   ○

7

back   belt   girl
○   ○   ○

4

stand   cry   swim
○   ○   ○

8

dog   dock   chin
○   ○   ○

GO ➡

9

wore

st

○   ○   ○

10

say

tr

○   ○   ○

11

rock

bl

○   ○   ○

12

low

cr

○   ○   ○

13

hum

dr

○   ○   ○

14

dish

f

○   ○   ○

GO

Test Yourself: Word Analysis

15	__ather	f ○	t ○	h ○
16	__im	st ○	ch ○	sw ○
17	__ar	f ○	j ○	m ○
18	__orse	h ○	l ○	t ○
19	l_f	oi ○	oa ○	ui ○
20	r__nge	e ○	i ○	a ○

GO

Unit 2 **Test Yourself: Word Analysis**

21  ○   ○   ○

22 ○   ○   ○

23 ○   ○   ○

24 ○    ○   ○

25  ○   ○    ○

GO

26

bike   rose   late

○   ○   ○

27

lead   best   beak

○   ○   ○

28

milk   must   mark

○   ○   ○

29

let   sand   miss

○   ○   ○

30

boil   room   smile

○   ○   ○

31

step   herd   pull

○   ○   ○

STOP

Look for an important word in the sentence that matches a picture.

S

For lunch, Rachel ate a banana.

○   ○   ○

1

Sara picks out clothes to wear. She chooses her new overalls.

○   ○   ○

2

Tim is making a snack. He gets food out of the cupboard.

○   ○   ○

3

Haley walked in the woods. She found a pretty feather.

○   ○   ○

Reading
Lesson 6b **Word Attack**

1

After washing the car, Lisa's mother parked in the garage.

◯   ◯   ◯

2

After it rained, we saw a rainbow.

◯   ◯   ◯

3

Connie put the dirty socks in the basket.

◯   ◯   ◯

4

David likes to sing into a microphone.

◯   ◯   ◯

STOP

Reading
Lesson 7a **Pictures**

Look at the picture when you answer the questions.

S Dad will _____ the picture.

    ○ paint   ○ frame   ○ hang   ○ buy

1 Tony is _____ his dad on the ladder.

    ○ watching   ○ working   ○ wearing   ○ wishing

2 Tony will hold the picture _____ Dad is ready for it.

    ○ because   ○ after   ○ where   ○ until

STOP

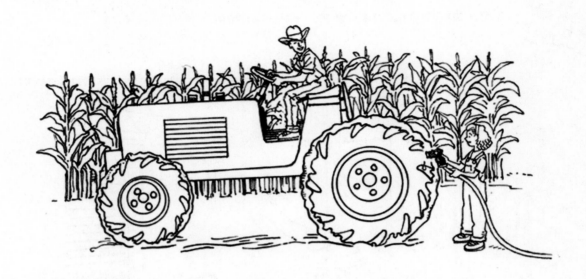

1 Suzy is next to Mr. Miller's _____.

○ bulldozer   ○ tractor   ○ truck   ○ car

2 Mr. Miller has been driving in the _____ fields.

○ muddy   ○ rainy   ○ empty   ○ frozen

3 Suzy will help Mr. Miller _____ the wheels.

○ stop   ○ turn   ○ water   ○ clean

STOP

S

> The cat jumped up on the chair. She walked in a circle. Then she sat down. After a minute, she jumped down on the floor.

What did the cat do first?

○ Walked in a circle

○ Jumped up on the chair

○ Sat down

Look back at the story to find the answer.

> It was time for Jack to go to school. He could not find his shoe. Jack looked all over the house. The shoe was nowhere.
> Jack's dog, Piper, came to Jack. Piper barked and went to the backyard. Jack followed him. Piper went into his doghouse. Jack looked inside. He was surprised. There was his shoe!
> "Now I know who took the shoe," Jack said.

1 What was Jack looking for?

○ His jacket

○ His shoe

○ His books

2 Where was Jack going?

○ School

○ The park

○ A baseball game

3 Where did Jack find his shoe?

○ Under the bed

○ In the closet

○ In a doghouse

GO

> Anna lived on a farm. Every day she collected eggs from the chickens.
>
> One spring day she went to the chicken house. There were no eggs. Then she heard a sound. She turned around. A chicken walked by. Ten yellow chicks ran behind her.
>
> Anna smiled. "That's where the eggs went!" she said.

4 **Where did Anna live?**

○ On a farm

○ In a city

○ On a boat

6 **How did Anna feel when she saw the chicks?**

○ Sad

○ Happy

○ Silly

5 **What was Anna's job?**

○ Mow the lawn

○ Set the table

○ Collect eggs

GO ➡

Mike's cat, Inky, is a strange cat. She loves to play outside in the yard. Inky's favorite outdoor game is "chase the stick." Mike throws a stick across the yard. Inky fetches it and brings it back.

Inky has two favorite indoor games. One is "catch the feather." Inky's toy is a string with a feather on the end. Mike pulls the feather across the floor. Inky chases it and grabs it with her mouth. She has pink feathers all over her face!

Inky's other favorite indoor game is "hide and seek." Inky takes small things like paper clips and pencils. She hides them under the couch. Whenever Mike needs a pencil, he looks under the couch.

7 **How many games does Inky like to play?**

○ One

○ Two

○ Three

9 **Which of these might Mike find under the couch?**

○ Furniture

○ Bicycle

○ Ballpoint pen

8 **Why is it strange that Inky likes to fetch a stick?**

○ Dogs like that game.

○ Mike throws it.

○ Birds like that game.

STOP

Emily's dad is a photographer. He loves to take pictures of animals. His dream is to take pictures of whales.

Last spring his wish came true. He and Emily were invited to ride on a big boat. The boat was filled with people studying whales. Emily's dad was hired to take pictures of the trip. They spent three weeks on the boat.

Every day Emily helped Dad with his cameras. Then they watched the sea. Soon the whales came. They were so big! Their huge tails slapped the water and made big splashes. Sometimes they swam next to the boat. One time Emily saw a baby whale.

1 What was Emily's dad's dream?

○ To ride on a boat

○ To take pictures of whales

○ To go on a trip with Emily

2 How long were Emily and her dad on the boat?

○ Three days

○ Three weeks

○ Three years

3 Why were the people on the boat?

○ They liked the ocean.

○ They studied whales.

○ They wanted to take pictures.

GO

> Birthdays were important in David's family. His sister Jenny had a birthday coming up. Jenny loved to read. But David did not have enough money to buy her a new book.
>
> David and his mother had an idea. He found what he needed in the basement. He borrowed Dad's tools. Then he got to work.
>
> Jenny's birthday came. She opened up her gift. It was a bookshelf. David had painted it red and yellow. They were Jenny's favorite colors.
>
> "I will hang this on my wall," Jenny said. "It is the best present I ever got."

4 **What celebration is this story about?**

○ Birthday
○ Wedding
○ Thanksgiving

5 **What is Jenny's favorite thing to do?**

○ Watch television
○ Read books
○ Play games

6 **Where did David find the paint he used on the bookshelf?**

○ At the store
○ Outside
○ In the basement

7 **Who helped David get the idea for the present?**

○ His mother
○ His father
○ His teacher

GO

My best friend, Amy, was in the hospital. She had hurt her foot. She couldn't come to school. We all missed her a lot. I knew that she missed us too.

One day our teacher got an idea. "We can't visit Amy all the time," she said. "But maybe there is a way to show her that we are thinking about her." The teacher gave each of us a big piece of paper. We filled the paper with nice sayings and pretty pictures.

The next week we visited Amy. She was so surprised to get our presents! Her mom put our big drawings on the wall. It made the room look beautiful.

"Get well soon, Amy," we said. "We all miss you."

8 **What is the story mostly about?**

○ Drawing pictures

○ Cheering up a friend

○ Visiting the hospital

10 **Why did Amy's mom put the drawings on the wall?**

○ To make the room nicer

○ To cover the windows

○ To remind her of Amy

9 **Why was Amy not in school?**

○ She was in the hospital.

○ She had moved.

○ She was home.

11 **What was wrong with Amy?**

○ She cut her hand.

○ She had a bad cold.

○ She hurt her foot.

Test Yourself: Reading

S

Wipe your feet on the mat.

○   ○   ○

1

Kelly hurt her thumb.

○   ○   ○

2

Nick and Wally looked at the toy train.

○   ○   ○

3

My friend has a pond. Her pet is a duck.

○   ○   ○

4 Joey is listening to his aunt play _____ music.

   ○ giant   ○ game   ○ giggle   ○ guitar

5 His _____ is moving in time with the music.

   ○ hand   ○ foot   ○ mouth   ○ head

6 Joey's sister is trying to _____ into the room.

   ○ sneak   ○ run   ○ throw   ○ scream

7 When Joey's aunt is done playing, she might give him a _____.

   ○ song   ○ gift   ○ job   ○ letter

STOP

Jonah's mom was at work. Jonah wanted to surprise her. He cleaned his room. He washed the dishes. He took out the trash.

Mom came home. She was surprised. "The house looks great!" she said. Jonah smiled.

Mom gave Jonah a present. It was a new game. Jonah was surprised. "Thank you for all your work," Mom said.

8 Where was Jonah's mom?

○ At home

○ At work

○ At school

10 What did Jonah's mom give him?

○ A shirt

○ A dog

○ A game

9 How did Jonah's mom feel when she came home?

○ Surprised

○ Foolish

○ Tired

GO

> Mom wanted to have a yard sale. "We have too many things," she said. "It's time to get rid of some things."
>
> Dad, Liz, and Penny got to work. They cleaned out the garage. Liz put all of her old toys in a box. Penny picked out the clothes that were too small. Mom set up tables in the yard. They put all of the things out to sell.
>
> "No one will buy this stuff!" Penny said.
>
> People came to the yard sale all day. Finally, it was over. "We worked hard and I am hungry," Mom said. She shook the money box. It was full. "We can buy a nice dinner," she said.

11 Why did Mom want to have a yard sale?

○ To buy a new table

○ To get rid of some things

○ To buy dinner

12 Who put clothes in the yard sale?

○ Liz

○ Mom

○ Penny

13 Why didn't Penny think anyone would buy their stuff?

○ She thought it was new.

○ She thought it was broken.

○ She thought it was junk.

14 How do you know the family sold many things?

○ The box was filled with money.

○ They cleaned out the garage.

○ Liz sold her old toys.

GO

Grandma was staying in a hotel for a while. Her house was being fixed. I liked to visit her. But the hotel was not the same as home. Grandma did not like it. Neither did I.

"What can we do?" I said. "You will be here for a few more weeks."

"I know," Grandma said. She whispered her plan to me. I grinned.

The next day Dad took me to Grandma's house. It seemed empty and sad without her. I found her collection of colored glass bottles. I took some perfume from her dresser. Then we went back to the hotel.

Grandma and I had so much fun hanging the bottles in front of her window. We put a drop of perfume in each one. The sun shone through the bottles and made colorful pictures on the floor.

"Now it smells like home," she said.

15 Why didn't Grandma and the child like the hotel?

○ It was too far away.

○ It cost too much money.

○ It wasn't the same as home.

16 What is this story mostly about?

○ Fixing a house that was old

○ Making a grandmother feel better

○ Staying in a hotel

17 How did the child get to Grandma's house?

○ Her mother took her.

○ Her father took her.

○ She walked by herself.

18 Why was the perfume so important?

○ It smelled like Grandma's house.

○ It was something that Dad liked.

○ It was a pretty color.

Listening
Lesson 9a **Listening Skills**

S

○   ○   ○

1

○   ○   ○

2

      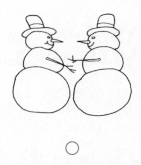

○   ○   ○

3

○   ○   ○

STOP

1

   ○

   ○

   ○

2

   ○

   ○

   ○

3

   ○

   ○

   ○

4

   ○

   ○

   ○

Test Yourself: Listening

S

○   ○   ○

1

○   ○   ○

2

○   ○   ○

3

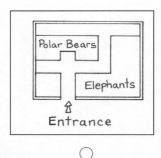 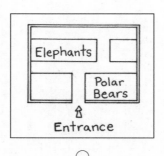

○   ○   ○

GO ➡

4

○ ○ ○

5

○ ○ ○

6

SKIRT OR PANTS

SOP **TOP** **SAT**

○ ○ ○

7

○ ○ ○

TIPS If you are not sure which answer is correct, take your best guess.

S

○   ○   ○

1

○   ○   ○

2

○   ○   ○

3

○   ○   ○

4

○   ○   ○

S

| dollar ○ | penny ○ | dime ○ | purse ○ |

1

| sister ○ | friend ○ | aunt ○ | father ○ |

2

| door ○ | window ○ | roof ○ | farm ○ |

3

| eyes ○ | nose ○ | see ○ | mouth ○ |

4

| dinner ○ | food ○ | lunch ○ | breakfast ○ |

5

| count ○ | four ○ | eight ○ | five ○ |

STOP

Language

Lesson 11a **Spelling**

Listen to the sentence while you look at the words.

Say each answer choice to yourself.

S

car ○   flatt ○   tire ○

5

what ○   boy ○   schout ○

1

water ○   runing ○   sink ○

6

rodes ○   wet ○   safe ○

2

air ○   open ○   windowe ○

7

girl ○   gess ○   name ○

3

trak ○   races ○   games ○

8

good ○   friends ○   figt ○

4

showe ○   began ○   noon ○

9

cach ○   ball ○   hand ○

STOP

42

Language
Lesson 11b Spelling

1

tose cold boots
○ ○ ○

2

stand bak line
○ ○ ○

3

animals lay gras
○ ○ ○

4

talks dinner mele
○ ○ ○

5

lok gold key
○ ○ ○

6

paye lady candles
○ ○ ○

7

baby rasch arm
○ ○ ○

8

clenes own brushes
○ ○ ○

9

dun feeding pony
○ ○ ○

10

one ligt house
○ ○ ○

STOP

Language
Lesson 12a Capitalization

The first word in a sentence should be capitalized.

Important words in a sentence should be capitalized.

S

○ The docker kids sent

○ a card to Grandma Betty

○ to celebrate Mother's Day.

3

○ Bring your umbrella

○ to school today. it looks like

○ it is going to start raining.

1

○ Have you gone skiing

○ before? Sasha and i go almost

○ every weekend in winter.

4

○ I asked my mom

○ if I could start taking music

○ lessons from mrs. Greer.

2

○ Jan and nick led a

○ group on a hike in the

○ mountains last summer.

5

○ The cat Garfield has a

○ comic strip named for him, but

○ the dog snoopy does not.

STOP

Language
Lesson 12b **Capitalization**

1
- ○   On Arbor Day, the
- ○ johnson family helped
- ○ Uncle Leroy plant a tree.

2
- ○   Joan and i are friends.
- ○ Both of us have relatives
- ○ who live in other countries.

3
- ○   There is a new pool
- ○ in town, so Fred and mike
- ○ are eager to go swimming.

4
- ○   It's a busy street.
- ○ look both ways before
- ○ you start to cross it.

5
- ○   I bought the book
- ○ at a garage sale and gave
- ○ it to mrs. Cook as a gift.

6
- ○   My pet fish Gus swims in
- ○ a straight line. My hermit
- ○ crab clyde crawls sideways.

STOP

 **TIPS**

Every sentence should end with punctuation.
Someone's initials should have a period.

S

○ The girls won their
○ first basketball game Then
○ they went to a pizza parlor.

3

○ Have you ever seen a lizard
○ with a bright blue belly My
○ friends and I have seen a few.

1

○ Aunt Barb has a cozy
○ basement We love to play and
○ watch movies down there.

4

○ Bang The wind blew
○ the screen door against the
○ back of Grandma's house.

2

○ James Taylor got the
○ nickname J T from his friends.
○ Now everyone calls him that.

5

○ Most of the students had
○ finished their paintings Bryce
○ was taking time with his.

STOP

1

○ The worker dug a small
○ hole in the ground Then he
○ planted three tiny seeds.

2

○ We helped Aunt Meg
○ clean her boat Tomorrow she
○ is taking us for a ride in it.

3

○ She had to find the
○ nearest U S Post Office
○ before five in the evening.

4

○ Will you go camping
○ this summer My friends
○ and I would like to invite you.

5

○ Plop Karl dropped a
○ spoonful of yogurt on the
○ front of his best shirt.

6

○ Many people have
○ one hobby Brianna has
○ five different ones.

STOP

Listen to the answers as you read along. Listen for a part of the answer that sounds like it is wrong.

S

- ○ Toby and Lila goes
- ○ shopping on Saturdays. Their
- ○ grandma goes with them.

3

- ○ Yuri's cousins wanted to ride
- ○ the bus home. Yuri asked them
- ○ if they had ever rided a bus.

1

- ○ I borrowed yours ruler.
- ○ You always let me use it
- ○ when I can't find my own.

4

- ○ Laird doesn't eat a lot
- ○ of candy. His parents
- ○ doesn't think it is a good habit.

2

- ○ Lisa told her dad she
- ○ needed new shoes. She needed
- ○ them ones for playing tennis.

5

- ○ After Clay found his batteries
- ○ were dead, he gone back to the
- ○ store to buy some new ones.

STOP

1

- ○ I haven't got no way to
- ○ get to school quickly. Both tires
- ○ on my bicycle need to be fixed.

2

- ○ Gil peeked inside the
- ○ garage and let out a happy cry.
- ○ The kittens they were so cute!

3

- ○ Jumping and spinning, the
- ○ team of dancers putting on a
- ○ great show for the crowd of people.

4

- ○ Rita and Heidi have been
- ○ bestest of friends ever since they
- ○ met in Mrs. Hashimoto's class.

5

- ○ We save our leftover
- ○ bread. On Saturdays, we take it
- ○ to the pond to feed the gooses.

6

- ○ After school, I and Tony
- ○ went to the park. We sat on a
- ○ bench and did our homework.

STOP

Test Yourself: Language

Unit 5

S

○   ○   ○

1

○   ○   ○

2

○   ○   ○

3

gold   silver   ring   copper
○   ○   ○   ○

4

pan   cook   kettle   dish
○   ○   ○   ○

5

run   ride   race   real
○   ○   ○   ○

GO ➤

6

drank ◯　　berry ◯　　puntch ◯

7

blose ◯　　trees ◯　　shake ◯

8

played ◯　　kik ◯　　yard ◯

9

found ◯　　peny ◯　　picked ◯

10

peke ◯　　inside ◯　　box ◯

11

wooden ◯　　blok ◯　　toy ◯

12

fence ◯　　poste ◯　　broken ◯

13

fisch ◯　　tank ◯　　bedroom ◯

14

wore ◯　　string ◯　　bedes ◯

15

flore ◯　　cabin ◯　　dirt ◯

GO →

Test Yourself: Language

16

- ○ Before the fireworks were lit,
- ○ the ryan family invited
- ○ Aunt Selma to come watch.

17

- ○ There were a lot of
- ○ leaves. Albert and i worked
- ○ all afternoon raking them.

18

- ○ Dara and katie make
- ○ decorations to sell at the
- ○ holiday gift fair at school.

19

- ○ Put our coats in the dryer.
- ○ they are soaked with water
- ○ after our long walk in the rain.

20

- ○ I went to the marketplace
- ○ and bought some flowers for
- ○ mr. Samson's birthday party.

21

- ○ My sister Wilma can
- ○ drive a car, but my brother
- ○ wayne is still too young.

GO

22

- ○ The bird collected bits
- ○ of grass and twigs Then it
- ○ began to build a nest.

23

- ○ Aunt Chrissie showed us
- ○ how to make bread Next she
- ○ will teach us to make noodles.

24

- ○ It was well past eleven in
- ○ the evening, but D D and I
- ○ were staying awake all night.

25

- ○ How many people can
- ○ sing and dance at the same
- ○ time My mom and I can.

26

- ○ Whoosh The kite that
- ○ was in Victor's hand caught
- ○ the wind like a paper rocket.

27

- ○ The bookshelf was filled
- ○ with all kinds of books Olivia
- ○ picked out three to borrow.

GO

28

- ○   Eddie and Orson is joining
- ○   the school band. Their teacher
- ○   is teaching them about music.

29

- ○   Mom asked me to help wash
- ○   hers car. The inside was clean,
- ○   but the outside was dirty.

30

- ○   Mr. Taylor says this here
- ○   house is a hundred years old.
- ○   I would like to live in it.

31

- ○   Dad went to buy more
- ○   milk, but luckily mom stopped
- ○   him. She had just buyed some.

32

- ○   Bart bought glasses for his
- ○   grandparents. Their eyes isn't
- ○   as strong as they used to be.

33

- ○   When Randy was in
- ○   the second grade, he grown
- ○   about three inches taller.

STOP

Mathematics Concepts

Lesson 15a **Mathematics Concepts**

Listen carefully while you look at the pictures.

S

○   ○   ○

3

○   ○   ○

1

⭐⭐⭐ ⭐⭐⭐⭐ ⭐⭐⭐⭐⭐⭐⭐

○   ○   ○

4

2 + 3 + ☐ = 9

3   4   9

○   ○   ○

2

sixteen

16   61   66

○   ○   ○

5

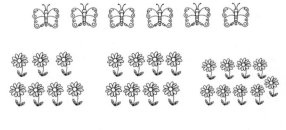

○   ○   ○

GO ➡

6

25   35   53

○   ○   ○

7

○   ○   ○

8

6 ☐ 2 = 4

=   +   −

○   ○   ○

9

○   ○   ○

10

26¢   36¢   52¢

○   ○   ○

11

20   29   42

○   ○   ○

GO ▶

12

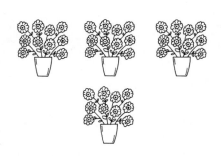

4	14	40
○	○	○

15

○   ○   ○   ○

13

○   ○   ○

16

9:00	12:00	3:00
○	○	○

14

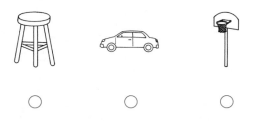

○   ○   ○

17

8	35	305
○	○	○

 STOP

1

2 + 2   8 − 5   8 + 3

○   ○   ○

2

○   ○   ○

3

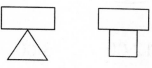

3 + 3 + 1   4 + 3 + 1   3 + 4 + 2

○   ○   ○

4

6   16   60

○   ○   ○

5

| 2 | 4 | | 8 | 10 |

5   6   7

○   ○   ○

6

○   ○   ○

GO

7

○   ○   ○

8

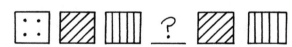

○   ○   ○

9

○ 2 + 3 = 1 + 4

○ 2 + 1 = 3 + 2

○ 4 + 2 = 3 + 1

10

○   ○   ○

11

22   29   38

○   ○   ○

12

1   2   7

○   ○   ○

13

○   ○   ○

16

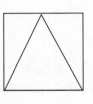 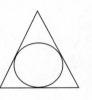

○   ○   ○

14

○   ○   ○

17

$$1 + 5 + \boxed{} = 8$$

1   2   6

○   ○   ○

15

thirteen

3   13   31

○   ○   ○

18

○   ○   ○

STOP

S

2   17   27

○   ○   ○

3

○   ○   ○

1

○   ○   ○

4

25¢   30¢   55¢

○   ○   ○

2

| 6 ☐ 2 = 8 |

=   +   −

○   ○   ○

5

17   25   31

○   ○   ○

GO

6

6   16   60

○   ○   ○

7

○   ○   ○

8

○   ○   ○

9

○   ○   ○   ○

10

1:15   1:30   6:00

○   ○   ○

11

42   402   420

○   ○   ○

GO

12

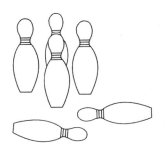

4 + 2   8 + 2   6 − 2

○   ○   ○

15

2   7   30

○   ○   ○

13

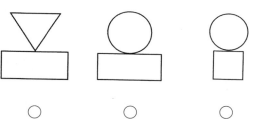

○   ○   ○

16

| 3 | 6 | 9 | 12 | |

15   17   19

○   ○   ○

14

3 + 5 + 5   4 + 3 + 1   3 + 4 + 2

○   ○   ○

17

○   ○   ○

GO

18

○ ○ ○

21

○ ○ ○

19

○ ○ ○

22

17   29   31

○ ○ ○

20

○ $2 + 3 = 3 + 5$

○ $2 + 1 = 3 + 1$

○ $4 + 2 = 2 + 4$

23

10   11   12

○ ○ ○

STOP

Unit 7 Mathematics Problems

Lesson 16a Mathematics Problems

TIPS Listen to the problem. Decide how you should solve it.

S1

1	2	3	N
○	○	○	○

S2

3	4	5	N
○	○	○	○

1

2	3	5	N
○	○	○	○

4

7	10	11	N
○	○	○	○

2

2	5	7	N
○	○	○	○

5

3	7	12	N
○	○	○	○

3

3	7	11	N
○	○	○	○

6

$3	$5	$13	N
○	○	○	○

GO ➡

7

3	4	10	N
○	○	○	○

10

1	2	6	N
○	○	○	○

8

6	7	9	N
○	○	○	○

11

1	2	5	N
○	○	○	○

9

1	3	5	N
○	○	○	○

12

4	6	8	N
○	○	○	○

STOP

Mathematics Problems

Lesson 16b **Mathematics Problems**

S1

| $2 - 1 =$ | $2 + 1 =$ | $3 + 2 =$ |
| ○ | ○ | ○ |

1

| $5 - 4 =$ | $3 + 2 =$ | $5 + 4 =$ |
| ○ | ○ | ○ |

2

| $10 - 2 =$ | $10 + 2 =$ | $8 + 2 =$ |
| ○ | ○ | ○ |

3

| $4 + 5 =$ | $5 - 4 =$ | $5 \times 4 =$ |
| ○ | ○ | ○ |

4

| $\$5 - \$5 =$ | $\$5 - \$2 =$ | $\$5 + \$2 =$ |
| ○ | ○ | ○ |

GO

S2 How many bananas are in the chart?
- ○ 3
- ○ 4
- ○ 5

6 How many more bananas than apples are there?
- ○ 1
- ○ 2
- ○ 3

5 If there were another orange, how many would there be in all?
- ○ 4
- ○ 5
- ○ 6

7 How many pears and apples are there all together?
- ○ 5
- ○ 6
- ○ 7

STOP

S1

1	2	3	N
○	○	○	○

3

3	8	10	N
○	○	○	○

1

1	7	9	N
○	○	○	○

4

6	7	9	N
○	○	○	○

2

2	4	7	N
○	○	○	○

5

2	7	10	N
○	○	○	○

GO ➤

Unit 7 **Test Yourself: Mathematics Problems**

S2

$1 + 1 =$ ○ $1 + 2 =$ ○ $2 + 3 =$ ○

6

$5 + 4 =$ ○ $5 + 9 =$ ○ $9 - 5 =$ ○

7

$5 + 4 =$ ○ $14 + 5 =$ ○ $14 - 5 =$ ○

8

$5 + 6 =$ ○ $5 \times 6 =$ ○ $6 - 5 =$ ○

9

$\$10 + \$6 =$ ○ $\$10 \times \$6 =$ ○ $\$10 - \$6 =$ ○

GO

Test Yourself: Mathematics Problems

10 **Which pet was chosen by 3 students?**
- ○ Dog
- ○ Cat
- ○ Fish

12 **Which pet was chosen by the most students?**
- ○ Dog
- ○ Bird
- ○ Cat

11 **Which pet was chosen by twice as many students as fish?**
- ○ Horse
- ○ Bird
- ○ Dog

13 **How many pets were chosen by more than three students?**
- ○ 1
- ○ 2
- ○ 3

STOP

TIPS Add and subtract carefully.

S1

1	4	5	N
○	○	○	○

3

13	14	19	N
○	○	○	○

1

4	6	10	N
○	○	○	○

4

0	17	18	N
○	○	○	○

2

6	9	19	N
○	○	○	○

5

10	25	35	N
○	○	○	○

GO →

S2

0	1	5	N
○	○	○	○

8

0	1	13	N
○	○	○	○

6

0	1	2	N
○	○	○	○

9

0	1	5	N
○	○	○	○

7

2	3	5	N
○	○	○	○

10

5	7	9	N
○	○	○	○

STOP

Unit 8

S
$$4$$
$$+\ 1$$

2 ○ 3 ○ 5 ○ N ○

4 $0 + 4 =$

0 ○ 1 ○ 5 ○ N ○

1 $5 - 4 =$

0 ○ 1 ○ 9 ○ N ○

5 $14 - 6 =$

2 ○ 8 ○ 10 ○ N ○

2
$$6$$
$$+\ 3$$

9 ○ 10 ○ 13 ○ N ○

6
$$16$$
$$-\ 4$$

2 ○ 6 ○ 8 ○ N ○

3
$$12$$
$$-\ 4$$

6 ○ 8 ○ 12 ○ N ○

7 $7 + 6 =$

13 ○ 14 ○ 16 ○ N ○

GO ▶

8

$$\begin{array}{r} 3 \\ 6 \\ + 8 \\ \hline \end{array}$$

10   17   18   N

○   ○   ○   ○

12 $45 - 2 =$

25   42   44   N

○   ○   ○   ○

9

$$\begin{array}{r} 19 \\ - 3 \\ \hline \end{array}$$

13   14   16   N

○   ○   ○   ○

13

$$\begin{array}{r} 31 \\ + 21 \\ \hline \end{array}$$

52   61   62   N

○   ○   ○   ○

10 $2 + 4 + 8 =$

12   13   16   N

○   ○   ○   ○

14 $24 - 6 =$

2   10   18   N

○   ○   ○   ○

11 $14 - 10 =$

1   4   5   N

○   ○   ○   ○

15

$$\begin{array}{r} 8 \\ + 12 \\ \hline \end{array}$$

11   20   21   N

○   ○   ○   ○

STOP

Test Yourself: Mathematics Computation

S

2	10	14	N
○	○	○	○

4

18	19	29	N
○	○	○	○

1

2	7	9	N
○	○	○	○

5

5	16	17	N
○	○	○	○

2

5	8	9	N
○	○	○	○

6

20	23	30	N
○	○	○	○

3

2	11	12	N
○	○	○	○

7

0	1	10	N
○	○	○	○

GO →

Test Yourself: Mathematics Computation

8

1	2	3	N
○	○	○	○

12

3	4	11	N
○	○	○	○

9

4	5	8	N
○	○	○	○

13

1	2	10	N
○	○	○	○

10

0	1	10	N
○	○	○	○

14

1	5	13	N
○	○	○	○

11

0	9	11	N
○	○	○	○

15

5	6	7	N
○	○	○	○

GO

16
$$\begin{array}{r} 3 \\ + 4 \\ \hline \end{array}$$

1   6   9   N

○   ○   ○   ○

20 $6 + 13 =$

7   19   20   N

○   ○   ○   ○

17
$$\begin{array}{r} 11 \\ - 2 \\ \hline \end{array}$$

9   13   21   N

○   ○   ○   ○

21
$$\begin{array}{r} 11 \\ - 5 \\ \hline \end{array}$$

6   7   16   N

○   ○   ○   ○

18 $0 + 2 =$

0   1   2   N

○   ○   ○   ○

22
$$\begin{array}{r} 15 \\ - 7 \\ \hline \end{array}$$

2   6   8   N

○   ○   ○   ○

19 $16 - 7 =$

6   7   8   N

○   ○   ○   ○

23 $6 + 4 =$

2   10   14   N

○   ○   ○   ○

STOP

Unit 9

Sources of Information

Lesson 18a **Sources of Information**

Listen carefully to the questions.

Carrot

Fig

Apple

Drink

Bread

Grapes

Egg

S1 Which picture should be at the very top of the page?

○ Apple

○ Bread

○ Egg

1 Which picture should be between the drink and the fig?

○ Apple

○ Grapes

○ Egg

2 Which picture should be the third one on the page?

○ Carrot

○ Fig

○ Bread

3 Which picture should be right after the apple?

○ Carrot

○ Bread

○ Drink

GO ▶

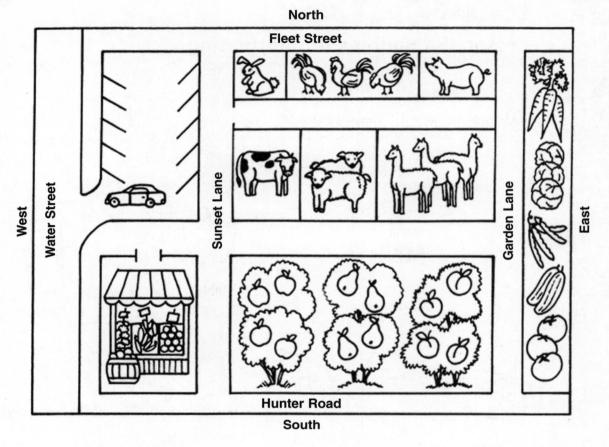

S2 Which animal has the biggest pen?

○ The pig

○ The llamas

○ The rabbit

4 Which is south of the sheep pen?

○ The chicken pen

○ The parking lot

○ The pear trees

5 Which direction do visitors go when they leave the parking lot and go to the fruit and vegetable shop?

○ South

○ East

○ West

6 What is north of the cow pen?

○ The sheep pen

○ The apple trees

○ The rabbit pen

7 What do visitors pass when they go from the barn to the fruit and vegetable shop?

○ The vegetable garden

○ The parking lot

○ The peach trees

8 Which is closest to Fleet Street?

○ The rabbit pen

○ The cow

○ The pear trees

GO →

Lesson 18a **Sources of Information**

Cc chest	
Ff funnel	
Jj jam	
Ll laundry	
Nn nails	
Pp package	
Ss sketch	
Ss soiled	

9 **Which is the most like a package?**
- ○ A chest
- ○ A funnel
- ○ A sketch

10 **How do you spell the name for a picture drawn quickly?**
- ○ skech
- ○ sketch
- ○ scetch

11 **Which of these would you be most likely to find in the refrigerator?**
- ○ laundry
- ○ nails
- ○ jam

12 **Which is most likely to be soiled?**
- ○ funnels
- ○ laundry
- ○ packages

13 **Which word fits best in the sentence "There was treasure inside the pirate's _____"?**
- ○ chest
- ○ funnel
- ○ sketch

14 **How do you spell the name of a box you get in the mail?**
- ○ packege
- ○ package
- ○ packidge

STOP

Unit 9

Sources of Information

Lesson 18b Sources of Information

Compare your answer with the map or table of contents.

N

Main Desk

Sitting area

Mrs. Coats

Art Room

Mr. Drill

Music Room

W

E

Hallway

Boys Restroom

Mrs. Eaton

Girls Restroom

Sidewalk

Mrs. Filbert

Library

Mr. Gibbs

S

---

1 **Where is Mr. Gibbs's room located?**

○ Across from the main desk

○ Next to the sitting area

○ Across from the library

2 **When the students walk from the main desk to the music room, what do they pass first?**

○ The sitting area

○ The restrooms

○ The library

3 **Which is west of the art room?**

○ Mrs. Coats's room

○ The music room

○ The sitting area

4 **Which of these is farthest from Mrs. Filbert's room?**

○ Mrs. Eaton's room

○ Mr. Drill's room

○ Mr. Gibbs's room

5 **Which direction would you walk from the library to Mrs. Filbert's room?**

○ West

○ North

○ East

GO

The Sea

CONTENTS

6 Which pages would tell you the most about the animals that live in the sea?

○ 3–6

○ 7–9

○ 13–15

7 Where should you begin reading to find out about people who work at sea?

○ 10

○ 13

○ 16

8 Which pages would tell you most about the weather at sea?

○ 10–12

○ 13–15

○ 16–18

9 Where should you begin reading to find a story about why there is a sea?

○ 3

○ 13

○ 19

10 Which pages would tell you most about colorful sea plants?

○ 7–9

○ 10–12

○ 13–15

11 Where should you begin reading to find out what a sailor does?

○ 10

○ 13

○ 16

STOP

Test Yourself: Sources of Information

S1 Which picture should be at the very top of the page?

○ Attic

○ Chair

○ Envelope

1 Which picture should be between the chair and the envelope?

○ Bed

○ Door

○ Fireplace

2 Which picture should be the second one on the page?

○ Chair

○ Door

○ Bed

3 Which picture should be right after the envelope?

○ Fireplace

○ Door

○ Grass

4 Which picture should be the last one on the page?

○ Attic

○ Grass

○ Envelope

5 Which picture should be right before the door?

○ Envelope

○ Grass

○ Chair

GO

Test Yourself: Sources of Information

North

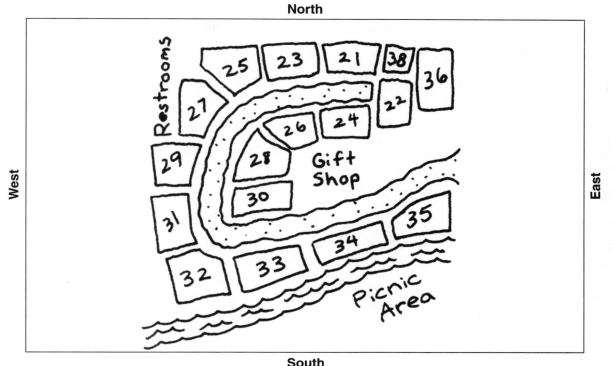

West

East

South

S2 **Which is the smallest campsite?**

○ Campsite 21

○ Campsite 38

○ Campsite 33

6 **Which campsite is south of the gift shop?**

○ Campsite 25

○ Campsite 34

○ Campsite 36

7 **Which direction do campers walk from campsite 25 to the restrooms?**

○ West

○ South

○ East

8 **What is south of campsite 32?**

○ The picnic area

○ Campsite 31

○ The river

9 **If you walked from the gift shop to the picnic area, which campsite might you pass through?**

○ Campsite 34

○ Campsite 36

○ Campsite 24

10 **Which campsite is closest to the entrance?**

○ Campsite 24

○ Campsite 29

○ Campsite 35

GO

Test Yourself: Sources of Information

Bb bucket	
Ff frame	
Ll loaf	
Ss sword	
Tt toast	
Vv vine	
Ww well	
Ww wrinkle	

11 Which is most like a bucket?

○ A well

○ A frame

○ A loaf

12 How do you spell the name for a line on the skin?

○ rinkle

○ wrinkle

○ wrinkel

13 Which of these would you be most likely to find in a backyard?

○ A sword

○ A frame

○ A vine

14 Which is most likely to be sliced?

○ A loaf

○ A well

○ A bucket

15 Which word fits best in the sentence "Around the picture was a carved _____"?

○ well

○ loaf

○ frame

16 How do you spell the name of a sharp metal weapon?

○ sowrd

○ sword

○ soard

GO ▶

Test Yourself: Sources of Information

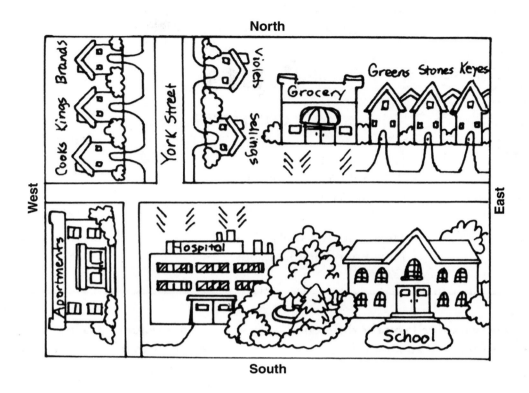

17 Where is the park located?

- ○ At the north end of the hospital
- ○ Next to the school
- ○ On the edge of the apartments

18 When the King children walk from home to school, what do they pass first?

- ○ The Cooks' house
- ○ The Greens' house
- ○ The Keyes' house

19 Which is west of the hospital?

- ○ The food store
- ○ The apartments
- ○ The school

20 Who lives farthest from the school?

- ○ The Brands
- ○ The Violets
- ○ The Stones

21 Who lives east of the food store?

- ○ The Sellings
- ○ The Brands
- ○ The Greens

22 Which direction would the Stone children walk to get to school?

- ○ East
- ○ North
- ○ South

Nuts

CONTENTS

23 Which pages would tell you the difference between a walnut and an almond?

○ 3–6

○ 7–8

○ 14–16

24 Where should you begin reading to find out if nuts grow on trees?

○ 7

○ 14

○ 17

25 Which pages would tell you most about nut farms?

○ 3–6

○ 14–16

○ 17–28

26 Where should you begin reading to find out how to include nuts in your everyday meals?

○ 3

○ 7

○ 9

27 Which pages would tell you why nuts are good for you?

○ 3–6

○ 7–8

○ 9–13

28 Where should you begin reading to find out about nuts grown in China?

○ 14

○ 17

○ 29

STOP

Science

Lesson 19a **Science Skills**

S

○   ○   ○

Listen carefully while you look at all of the pictures. When you find the picture you think is correct, put your finger on it. Then mark the circle for your answer.

1

○   ○   ○

2

○   ○   ○

GO

3

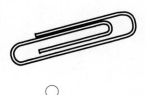

◯

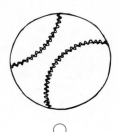

◯

◯

4

◯

◯

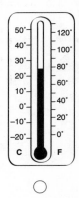

◯

5

◯

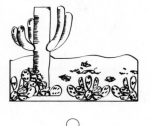

◯

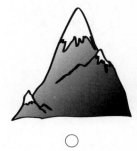

◯

6

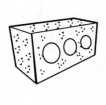

◯

◯

◯

GO ➡

7

 ○    ○    ○

8

 ○    ○    ○

9

 ○    ○    ○

10

 ○   ○    ○

GO

11

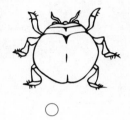 ○

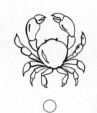 ○

 ○

12

 ○

 ○

 ○

13

 ○

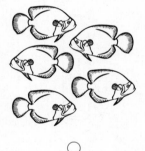 ○

 ○

14

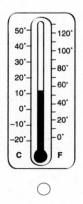 ○

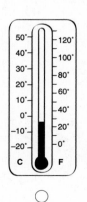 ○

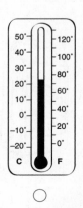 ○

GO

15

 ○    ○    ○

16

 ○   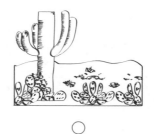 ○    ○

17

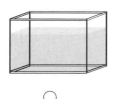 ○   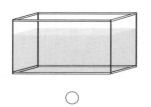 ○   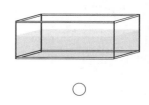 ○

18

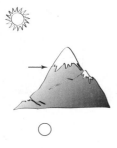 ○   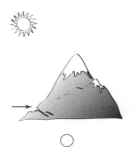 ○   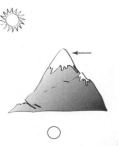 ○

GO

19

○   ○   ○

20

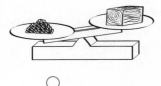 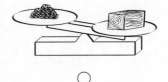 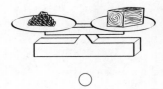

○   ○   ○

21

○   ○   ○

22

○   ○   ○

STOP

S

○   ○   ○

If you aren't sure which answer is correct, take your best guess. After you mark your answer, get ready for the next question.

1

○   ○   ○

2

○   ○   ○

GO ➡

Unit 10 Lesson 19b **Science Skills**

3

○   ○   ○

4

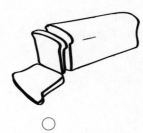   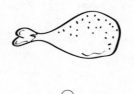   

○   ○   ○

5

○   ○   ○

6

○   ○   ○

GO

7

○   ○   ○

8

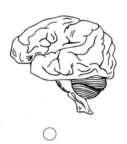   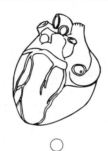   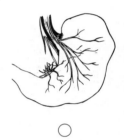

○   ○   ○

9

○   ○   ○

10

○   ○   ○

GO ➡

11

 ○    ○    ○

12

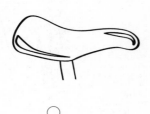 ○    ○   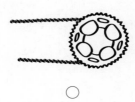 ○

13

 ○    ○    ○

14

 ○    ○    ○

GO ▶

15

○

○

○

16

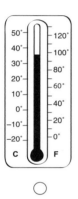
○

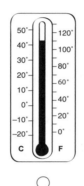
○

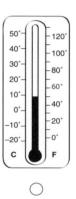
○

17

○

○

○

18

○

○

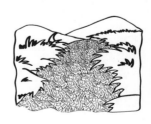
○

GO ▶

19

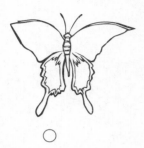 ○

 ○

 ○

20

 ○

 ○

 ○

21

  ○

 ○

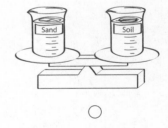 ○

22

 ○

 ○

 ○

STOP

S

○   ○   ○

1

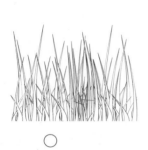      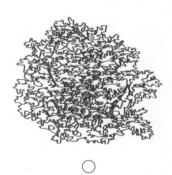

○   ○   ○

2

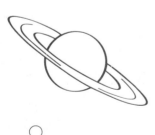      

○   ○   ○

GO

3

○ ○ ○

4

○ ○ ○

5

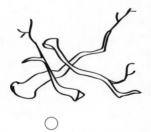  

○ ○ ○

6

○ ○ ○

GO

Unit 10   Test Yourself: Science

7

○   ○   ○

8

○   ○   ○

9

○   ○   ○

10

○   ○   ○   GO ▶

11

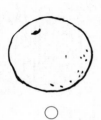 ○    ○    ○

12

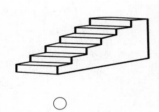 ○   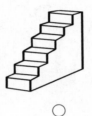 ○   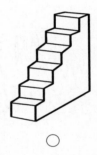 ○

13

 ○    ○    ○

14

 ○   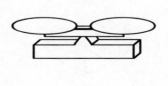 ○    ○

GO

15

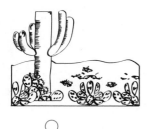 ○

 ○

 ○

16

 ○

 ○

 ○

17

 ○

 ○

 ○

18

 ○

 ○

 ○

GO

Unit 10

Test Yourself: Science

19

   ○

   ○

   ○

20

   ○

   ○

   ○

21

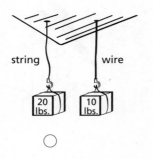   ○

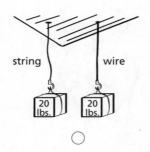   ○

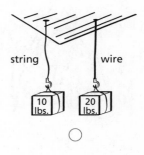   ○

22

   ○

   ○

   ○

GO ▶

106

Test Yourself: Science

23

 ○  ○  ○

24

 ○  ○ 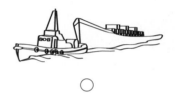 ○

25

 ○  ○  ○

26

 ○  ○  ○

GO

27

○   ○   ○

28

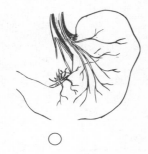   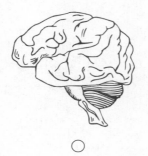   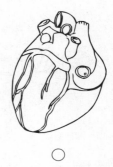

○   ○   ○

29

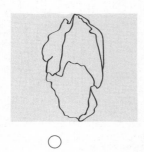   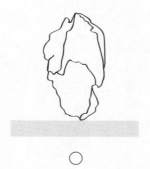   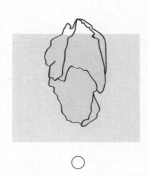

○   ○   ○

30

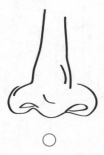   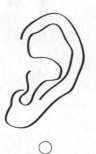   

○   ○   ○

GO

Unit 10   **Test Yourself: Science**

31

    ○   ○   ○

32

    ○   ○   ○

33

    ○   ○   ○

34

      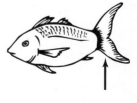

    ○   ○   ○

Test Yourself: Science

35

   ○

   ○

   ○

36

   ○

   ○

   ○

37

   ○

   ○

   ○

38

   ○

   ○

   ○

STOP

S

- ○ clump
- ○ cloud
- ○ camp
- ○ cliff

3

- ○ stack
- ○ bend
- ○ lean
- ○ pile

1

- ○ heal
- ○ comfort
- ○ tease
- ○ visit

4

- ○ web
- ○ nest
- ○ den
- ○ cave

2

- ○ listen
- ○ sing
- ○ read
- ○ watch

5

- ○ feathers
- ○ ears
- ○ horns
- ○ mane

STOP

6

A quiet voice is a …

○ whisper   ○ shout   ○ yell   ○ swallow

7

To be worried is to be …

○ tired   ○ nervous   ○ alone   ○ comfortable

8

To look quickly is to …

○ blink   ○ grin   ○ rip   ○ peek

9

Something that is not real is …

○ pretend   ○ easy   ○ wonderful   ○ terrible

10

To go up a ladder is to …

○ walk   ○ dance   ○ spin   ○ climb

11

To become different is to …

○ agree   ○ think   ○ change   ○ promise

STOP

S1

glow   grow   roam
 ○   ○   ○

S2

stay   slow   blue
 ○   ○   ○

1

snail   lean   hair
 ○   ○   ○

5

dump   just   bank
 ○   ○   ○

2

about   inside   ending
 ○   ○   ○

6

said   deck   ride
 ○   ○   ○

3

play   price   lunch
 ○   ○   ○

7

with   catch   past
 ○   ○   ○

4

ink   are   ant
 ○   ○   ○

8

rich   dish   sink
 ○   ○   ○

GO

9

rag
fl

○ ○ ○

10

say
h

○ ○ ○

11

tail
sn

○ ○ ○

12

tell
sh

○ ○ ○

13

sunk
tr

○ ○ ○

14

sick
br

○ ○ ○

GO

15	 __asket	p ○	b ○	d ○
16	 __oat	l ○	c ○	f ○
17	 __ar	g ○	y ○	j ○
18	 __ony	p ○	l ○	r ○
19	 p__cket	i ○	o ○	a ○
20	 cr__l	aw ○	oo ○	ai ○

GO

21

 ○   ○   ○

22

 ○   ○   ○

23

 ○   ○    ○

24

kite   main   job
○   ○   ○

25

cold   great   side
○   ○   ○

26

lunch   fruit   dive
○   ○   ○

STOP

Test Practice

Test 3 **Reading**

S

When she rides her bike, Mary always wears a helmet.

○

○

○

1

Nick uses a computer. He types on the keyboard.

○

○

○

2

Dylan painted a picture. Then he cleaned his brushes.

○

○

○

3

John went to the zoo. He saw a monkey.

○

○

○

4   Max and Annie are playing in the ———.

○ bathtub   ○ pool   ○ park   ○ driveway

5   Max is holding a ———.

○ hose   ○ bucket   ○ towel   ○ sprinkler

6   Annie is ——— Max with water.

○ scaring   ○ shouting   ○ shaking   ○ splashing

STOP

Jody's mother loves to spin her own yarn. First, she buys fluffy wool from a farm. Then she cleans it and combs it into long pieces. She puts the pieces through a spinning wheel. The wheel twists the wool tight and makes yarn.

After Jody's mother is finished spinning, she knits with the yarn. She makes mittens, scarves, and socks. Her wool socks keep Jody's feet warm in winter. Jody loves the socks her mom makes.

7 **Where does Jody's mom get her wool?**

○ From a store
○ From her friend
○ From a farm

9 **Which of these did mother make for Jody?**

○ Scarves
○ Mittens
○ Socks

8 **What does the spinning wheel do?**

○ Rolls on the ground
○ Twists the wool into yarn
○ Makes mittens

GO

It was the last day of school. Sarah, Josh, and the other students couldn't wait for school to be out for the summer. Their class was noisy and restless. Suddenly the door opened. The principal walked in.

"Sarah and Josh, come with me," she said. They followed the principal down the hall.

"Are we in trouble?" whispered Josh. Sarah didn't know. She was scared.

They went to the library. There were many other children inside. There was a cake and punch.

"This is a special party," the principal said. "I want to thank you all for having perfect attendance all year!" Everyone clapped and cheered. Sarah and Josh clapped too.

10 **Who came for Sara and Josh?**
○ The teacher
○ The principal
○ Their friends

11 **What was the surprise?**
○ A game
○ A day off
○ A party

12 **Why were the children noisy and restless?**
○ They didn't have any homework.
○ The teacher was sick.
○ They wanted to start their vacation.

13 **What was true about all the children in the library?**
○ They all had perfect attendance.
○ They were library helpers.
○ They were friends.

GO

I went to Aunt Lily's house last week to cheer her up. I knew she was sad because her son had moved away. He had gotten married and had a new job.

I found a big, old book at Aunt Lily's house. It was tied with string. Inside I found a red rose pressed in the pages.

"Your cousin Joe gave me that rose a long time ago," Aunt Lily told me. "Every time I see red roses I think of him."

The next time I went to Aunt Lily's house I took her some roses.

"The red roses are so you will remember Joe," I said.

"What is the yellow rose for?" Aunt Lily asked.

"That one is so that you will think of me," I said.

14 **What is this story mostly about?**

○ Remembering people you love
○ Buying flowers for the kitchen
○ Visiting family

15 **Why did Aunt Lily press the rose in the book?**

○ To keep the flower fresh
○ To remind her of Joe
○ To mark a page

16 **Why did the child think Aunt Lily would forget Joe?**

○ He was away at school.
○ He had moved.
○ He was coming home soon.

17 **How do red roses remind her of Joe?**

○ They grew in his yard.
○ They are pretty.
○ He gave her one long ago.

STOP

Test Practice
Test 4 **Listening**

S

   ○   ○   ○

1

   ○      ○      ○

2

   ○   ○   ○

3

dollar   penny   dime   purse
○   ○   ○   ○

4

sew   thread   rope   string
○   ○   ○   ○

5

up   stand   down   around
○   ○   ○   ○

STOP

S

found ○   peny ○   picked ○

1

peke ○   inside ○   box ○

2

wooden ○   blok ○   toy ○

3

fence ○   poste ○   broken ○

4

fisch ○   tank ○   bedroom ○

5

wore ○   string ○   bedes ○

6

flore ○   cabin ○   dirt ○

7

lamp ○   brigt ○   read ○

8

reatch ○   top ○   shelf ○

9

new ○   shoos ○   tight ○

GO →

10

○ The carver family spends
○ every Independence Day at
○ a campsite near the beach.

11

○ Where is the nearest
○ bank? My mom and i have
○ not been able to find it.

12

○ Matt and anna are
○ members of a postcard club
○ that meets once a month.

13

○ The street cleaner asked
○ people to move their cars Then
○ he swept and washed the street.

14

○ We planted a strawberry
○ patch with Uncle Shelby Soon we
○ will be eating fresh strawberries.

15

○ The new kid on the block
○ is O P Barnes, and Saturday at
○ six he is joining us for dinner.

GO

16

○   I haven't never won a

○ prize in a contest. I keep

○ hoping that someday I will.

17

○   Mom could not believe

○ what she saw in the car mirror.

○ The kids they were sleeping!

18

○   Frank watched how

○ his dad made his famous

○ pancakes. Mixed and fried.

19

○   Ella was hungry, and

○ the warm soup made her

○ stomach feel much gooder.

20

○   A group of deers stood

○ in the middle of the large

○ meadow behind the barn.

21

○   Sundays are my favorite

○ days. That is when I and Luis

○ work on our backyard tree fort.

STOP

S

○   ○   ○

3

  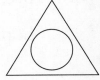

○   ○   ○

1

○   ○   ○

4

$$4 + 3 + \square = 10$$

3   4   9

○   ○   ○

2

| fourteen |

4   12   14

○   ○   ○

5

○   ○   ○

GO →

6

37   27   73

○   ○   ○

9

○   ○   ○

7

○   ○   ○

10

45¢   3¢   27¢

○   ○   ○

8

$$4 \ \square \ 5 = 9$$

=   +   –

○   ○   ○

11

31   37   47

○   ○   ○

GO

12

10   20   30

◯   ◯   ◯

13

◯   ◯   ◯

14

◯   ◯   ◯

15

◯   ◯   ◯   ◯

16

4:30   6:00   1:30

◯   ◯   ◯

17

7   17   107

◯   ◯   ◯

STOP

Test Practice
Test 7 Mathematics Problems

S

1	2	4	N
○	○	○	○

4

7	8	10	N
○	○	○	○

1

2	3	9	N
○	○	○	○

5

8	10	18	N
○	○	○	○

2

2	5	7	N
○	○	○	○

6

$3	$4	$10	N
○	○	○	○

3

4	10	12	N
○	○	○	○

7

0	1	4	N
○	○	○	○

GO →

8

$4 - 3 =$ $4 + 3 =$ $7 - 3 =$

○   ○   ○

9

$9 - 3 =$ $3 + 9 =$ $12 + 3 =$

○   ○   ○

10

$11 + 3 =$ $14 - 3 =$ $11 - 3 =$

○   ○   ○

11

$4 + 3 =$ $4 \times 3 =$ $4 - 3 =$

○   ○   ○

12

$\$20 - \$10 =$ $\$20 + \$10 =$ $\$20 - \$20 =$

○   ○   ○

GO ➡

Test 7 **Mathematics Problems**

Number of Birds Counted in One Week

	School	Park
Monday	9	12
Tuesday	5	9
Wednesday	18	14
Thursday	6	4
Friday	3	9

13 **How many birds were counted in the park on Wednesday?**
- ○ 9
- ○ 12
- ○ 14

14 **The number of birds counted in the park on Tuesday was the same as the number of birds counted at school on which day?**
- ○ Monday
- ○ Tuesday
- ○ Thursday

15 **On which day were the fewest number of birds counted in the park?**
- ○ Wednesday
- ○ Thursday
- ○ Friday

16 **How many more birds were counted at school than in the park on Wednesday?**
- ○ 3
- ○ 4
- ○ 6

Test Practice
Test 8 Mathematics Computation

Unit 11

S

5	7	16	N
○	○	○	○

4

2	3	10	N
○	○	○	○

1

9	10	14	N
○	○	○	○

5

5	7	11	N
○	○	○	○

2

10	12	14	N
○	○	○	○

6

1	5	10	N
○	○	○	○

3

10	15	25	N
○	○	○	○

7

4	6	14	N
○	○	○	○

GO →

8

$$
\begin{array}{r}
3 \\
+\ 6 \\
\hline
\end{array}
$$

3	8	9	N
○	○	○	○

12

$$
\begin{array}{r}
16 \\
-\ 7 \\
\hline
\end{array}
$$

1	11	9	N
○	○	○	○

9

$$
\begin{array}{r}
12 \\
-\ 2 \\
\hline
\end{array}
$$

2	10	22	N
○	○	○	○

13

$$7 + 9 =$$

16	17	19	N
○	○	○	○

10

$$0 + 9 =$$

0	10	90	N
○	○	○	○

14

$$4 + 14 =$$

10	17	24	N
○	○	○	○

11

$$14 - 8 =$$

6	8	22	N
○	○	○	○

15

$$
\begin{array}{r}
11 \\
-\ 9 \\
\hline
\end{array}
$$

1	2	20	N
○	○	○	○

STOP

Test Practice

Test 9 **Sources of Information**

Can

Fork

Apron

Dish

Broom

Glass

Easel

S1 Which picture should be at the very top of the page?

- ○ Apron
- ○ Can
- ○ Easel

1 Which picture should be between the broom and the dish?

- ○ Fork
- ○ Glass
- ○ Can

2 Which picture should be the second one on the page?

- ○ Can
- ○ Broom
- ○ Dish

3 Which picture should be right after the easel?

- ○ Broom
- ○ Fork
- ○ Apron

4 Which picture should be the last one on the page?

- ○ Fork
- ○ Broom
- ○ Glass

5 Which picture should be right before the fork?

- ○ Easel
- ○ Glass
- ○ Dish

Test 9 **Sources of Information**

North

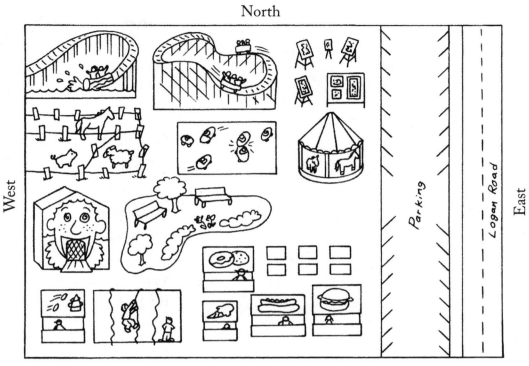

West · Parking · Logan Road · East

South

S2 **Which is the smallest stand in the food court?**

○ The ice cream stand

○ The bakery stand

○ The hamburger stand

6 **Which of these is south of the bumper cars?**

○ The carousel

○ The petting zoo

○ The climbing wall

7 **Which direction do people go when they leave the food court and walk to the art show?**

○ East

○ North

○ South

8 **What is south of the fun house?**

○ The bumper cars

○ The rest area

○ The ring toss

9 **What does John pass when he goes from the log ride to the rest area?**

○ The roller coaster

○ The carousel

○ The food court

10 **Which is closest to Logan Road?**

○ The petting zoo

○ The bumper cars

○ The hamburger stand

GO

Test 9 Sources of Information

Bb bundle	
Cc corner	
Gg glitter	
Mm mystery	
Nn necklace	
Oo officer	
Pp puzzle	
Ss stampede	

11 Which is the most like a mystery?
- ○ A puzzle
- ○ A corner
- ○ A bundle

12 How do you spell the name for something that is tied up?
- ○ bundel
- ○ bundil
- ○ bundle

13 Which of these would you be most likely to see at a ranch?
- ○ An officer
- ○ A stampede
- ○ A necklace

14 Which is most likely to glitter?
- ○ A necklace
- ○ A puzzle
- ○ A corner

15 Which word fits best in the sentence "Jack stood on the _____ and waited for his ride"?
- ○ bundle
- ○ corner
- ○ stampede

16 How do you spell what the stars do at night?
- ○ gliter
- ○ glider
- ○ glitter

GO →

Turtles

CONTENTS

17 Which pages would tell you most about what different turtles look like?

- ○ 2–4
- ○ 5–7
- ○ 8–9

18 Where should you begin reading to find out about when the first turtles lived?

- ○ 5
- ○ 8
- ○ 15

19 Which pages would tell you most about how bably turtles are born?

- ○ 2–4
- ○ 5–7
- ○ 10–11

20 Where should you begin reading to find out about what turtles eat?

- ○ 5
- ○ 12
- ○ 15

21 Which pages would tell you most about where turtles live?

- ○ 5–7
- ○ 8–9
- ○ 10–11

22 Where should you begin reading to find out how to protect turtles?

- ○ 2
- ○ 8
- ○ 15

STOP

Test Practice

Test 10 **Science**

S

○ ○ ○

1

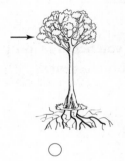  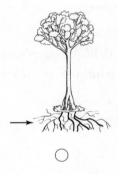

○ ○ ○

2

 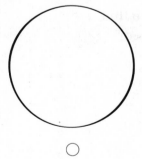 

○ ○ ○

GO

138

3

      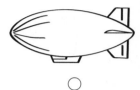

○   ○   ○

4

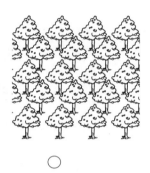      

○   ○   ○

5

○   ○   ○

6

○   ○   ○

GO

7

 ○    ○    ○

8

 ○    ○    ○

9

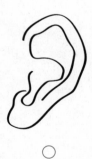 ○    ○    ○

10

 ○    ○    ○

GO

Test 10 **Science**

11

  ○

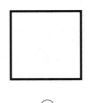 ○

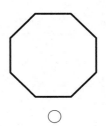 ○

12

 ○

 ○

 ○

13

 ○

 ○

 ○

14

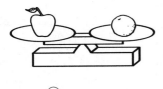 ○

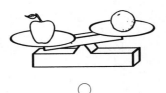 ○

 ○

GO

15

  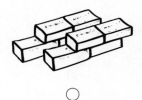

○   ○   ○

16

○   ○   ○

17

○   ○   ○

18

○   ○   ○   **GO** ➤

19

　　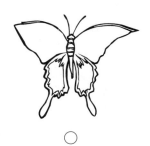　　

○　　　　　　　○　　　　　　　○

20

○　　　　　　　○　　　　　　　○

21

○　　　　　　　○　　　　　　　○

22

○　　　　　　　○　　　　　　　○

GO

23

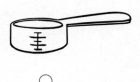 ○

 ○

 ○

24

 ○

 ○

 ○

25

 ○

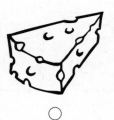 ○

 ○

26

 ○

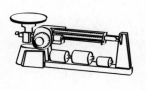 ○

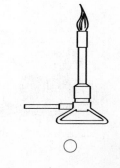 ○

GO

Unit 11

Test 10 **Science**

27

 ○    ○    ○

28

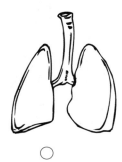 ○   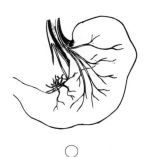 ○   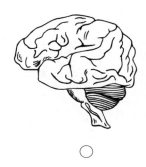 ○

29

 ○    ○    ○

30

 ○    ○    ○

Test 10 **Science**

31

○   ○   ○

32

○   ○   ○

33

○   ○   ○

34

○   ○   ○   **GO**

35

 ○

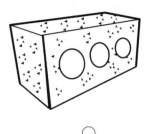 ○

 ○

36

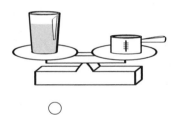 ○

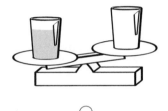 ○

 ○

37

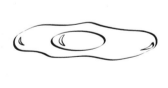 ○

 ○

 ○

38

 ○

 ○

 ○

STOP